AMERICA THE BEAUTIFUL
VS
AMERICA NOT SO BEAUTIFUL - 2025

PW WILLIAMS

Copyright © 2025 by PW Williams

All rights reserved. No part of this book may be reproduced, distributed, or transmitted in any form or by any means, including photocopying, recording, or other electronic or mechanical methods, without the prior written permission of the publisher.

ISBN: 979-8-89397-568-0

Edition: First

Published by AMZ Kindle Direct Publications

A Patriot Song: "America the Beautiful" written 1895 VS "America Not So Beautiful" NOW

WHY?

PROJECT 2025 AND MUCH MORE!

Introduction

Trump and America: Not So Beautiful

The Promise of Change

Donald Trump's presidential campaign was built on the promise of radical change. His slogan, "Make America Great Again," resonated with millions of voters who felt left behind by globalization, economic shifts, and perceived political elitism. Trump positioned himself as a champion of the common man, willing to take on entrenched interests and restore American prosperity and pride.

Contentious Policies and Decisions

Trump's administration enacted a range of policies that sparked intense debate. From immigration reforms, including the infamous travel ban and border wall project, to tax cuts primarily benefiting corporations and the wealthy, each decision was controversial.

His approach to international relations, characterized by a withdrawal from multilateral agreements and confrontational stances with allies and adversaries alike, further strained America's global relationships.

Immigration and Border Security

One of Trump's most contentious policies was his stance on immigration. The travel ban targeting predominantly Muslim countries and the separation of families at the southern border drew widespread condemnation. The construction of the border wall became a symbol of his administration's hardline approach, intended to curb illegal immigration but criticized for its humanitarian impact.

Economic Policies

Trump's economic policies included significant tax cuts, deregulation, and renegotiating trade deals. While proponents argued these measures would stimulate the economy and create jobs, critics highlighted the disproportionate benefits to the wealthy and potential long-term fiscal challenges. The renegotiated NAFTA, now known as the USMCA, aimed to create fairer trade terms but faced scrutiny over its effectiveness in protecting American jobs.

International Relations

Trump's foreign policy was marked by unpredictability and assertiveness. His administration's withdrawal from the Paris Agreement on climate change and the Iran nuclear deal drew criticism from global leaders and environmental advocates. Relations with traditional allies were strained, as Trump frequently clashed with NATO members and questioned the value of longstanding alliances. Conversely, his engagement with North Korea and trade negotiations with China were seen as bold moves, though their outcomes remain mixed.

A Divisive Public Figure

Trump's presidency was not only characterized by policies but also by his persona. His use of social media, particularly Twitter, to communicate directly with the public and attack opponents was unprecedented. The frequent dissemination of misinformation and incendiary rhetoric polarized the nation, leading to deep political and social divides. The media landscape was transformed as outlets either aligned with or opposed to his administration, further entrenching partisan perspectives.

The Legacy of Trump's Presidency

As Trump left office in January 2021, his legacy remained intensely debated. Supporters lauded his efforts to shake up the status quo and prioritize American interests. Critics warned of lasting damage to America's democracy, rule of law, and social cohesion, citing his rhetoric, challenges to election results, and divisive policies.

"America the Beautiful" is a heartfelt and patriotic song cherished across the United States of America. Written in 1895, the lyrics were penned by Katharine Lee Bates, a distinguished American writer and professor. Samuel A. Ward composed the evocative music, whose melody perfectly complements Bates's stirring words.

Over the years, "America the Beautiful" has emerged as one of the most beloved patriotic songs in the United States, capturing the essence of the nation's spirit and landscape. This timeless anthem continues to resonate with Americans, reflecting their pride and love for their country.

Today, in 2025, we can no longer say America the Beautiful or Make America Great Again.

America is not so beautiful or great today in 2025. We unravel the complex layers of the American dream, exploring the disparity between the idealized vision of a utopian society and the often-harsh realities of life in the United States in the year 2025. This book challenges us to look beyond the star-spangled façade of America the Beautiful and examine the socioeconomic and environmental issues that undermine the nation's promise and laws of the land. We delve into the historical roots of these issues, from colonialism and slavery to modern policies that perpetuate inequality.

Through compelling narratives and insightful analysis, the book highlights the voices of those often marginalized, calling for a reevaluation of what it truly means to be an American.

Amidst the critique, America Not So Beautiful also explores stories of resilience and hope, showcasing the efforts of communities striving for a more equitable and just society by examining both the darkness of the GOP and the light of the American people. This book aims to spark a conversation about America's future and the potential for positive change. Checks and balances that once defined American democracy seem to erode the GOP-controlled Congress, once a bastion of debate and oversight, but now echo the president's will.

Everyone who is nominated by the President to be part of his cabinet must go through a confirmation process. Each candidate is questioned by the House of Representatives, which asks questions regarding the position and a little background about themselves. Each congressman or congresswoman would ask specific questions about the position to see if the person is qualified. You would have a Democrat ask a question or a Republican ask a question, which is generally the procedure. A smooth run confirmation, year 2025; it is very different from the reason the Republicans control the House of Representatives plus the Senate. What does that mean? If the Democrats question a candidate for a position and feel this person does not qualify for the position, they will cast a no vote.

On the other hand, Republicans vote yes, even though the person does not have the proper experience or qualifications; the majority of the Republicans vote yes because Trump tells them to vote yes. Trump is abandoning his fundamental role. He is acting as if the White House is his business, and he tells his employees what to do, who are congressmen and senators; the Majority of the congressmen and senators are Republicans. Imagine if the people had rallied behind a humble servant like Kamala Harris, who presents herself as a grounded political figure, despite her faults. While she is not without her criticisms, power-hungry, I do not believe she has any inclination toward authoritarianism or dictatorial practices. I am confident that she will not engage in policies that would harm the most vulnerable, such as exacerbating poverty, dismantling Social Security, or eliminating vital programs like Medicaid and Medicare. Furthermore, I believe she would not resort to drastic measures that would result in the loss of thousands of government jobs.

Having served as a prosecuting attorney, Harris understands the importance of due process and accountability. It is reasonable to assume that she would rigorously evaluate the backgrounds of individuals, including billionaires or other influential figures, before allowing them any proximity to the White House. This would likely include thorough confirmation hearings and mandatory security clearances to ensure the integrity of her administration.

I also have faith that Harris would treat all individuals with fairness, not because she is a Democrat, but because I believe in what is right. I am not with either party. I know she would adhere to the rule of law and fulfill her duty to uphold and defend the United States Constitution. Her commitment to these principles reinforces my belief that she would maintain strong, cooperative relationships with our allies while firmly opposing any actions that would bolster our adversaries. Instead, Americans voted for a madman who is on the brink of dictatorship, a grim reminder of the lessons of the past.

America is heading towards a dictatorship because, let's look at the past. In the year 1933, Adolf Hitler was an Austrian-born German politician. His birth name was Adolf Schickelgruber. His father, Alois, changed his name to Adolf Hitler in 1876. Adolf Hitler was a dictator of Nazi Germany from 1933 until his suicide in 1945. He rose to power as the leader of the Nazi party, aka the GOP today in the year 2025.

Through his deceitful lies and imagination, he became the chancellor in 1933 and took the title of Führer und Reichskanzler in 1934. Hitler pledged to restore prosperity and create civil order (by crushing industrial strikes and street demonstrations by others who opposed him, including communists and socialists), eliminate the influence of Jewish financiers, and make the fatherland once again a world power (make America great again).

Sounds similar?

The current system of checks and balances in the United States is increasingly ineffective. Historically, Congress was intended to be a robust counterweight to the executive branch, ensuring that no single entity could gain excessive power. What that means is something that has a separate, distinct existence and objective or conceptual reality.

As we move towards 2025, there has been a significant shift in the political landscape, particularly in the behavior of Congress in relation to presidential policies. While not every member of Congress consistently aligns with the agenda set forth by the President, there is a notable trend among Republican lawmakers who largely support and adhere to these policies.

This environment creates a complex dynamic where Democrats are compelled to navigate the legislative process with a commitment to procedural integrity, often striving to engage in bipartisanship and uphold established norms when proposing new legislation or collaborating on issues of national importance.

In stark contrast, the Republican Party appears willing to prioritize allegiance to President Trump over traditional legislative processes. This tendency to sidestep established procedures in favor of expediting support for the President's initiatives raises alarming questions about the increasing concentration of power within the executive branch.

Consequently, this not only affects the balance of power among the branches of government but also poses risks to democratic norms and the overall effectiveness of governance. The overarching concern is that such behavior could lead to an erosion of institutional checks and balances, further entrenching partisan divisions within Congress.

As voters approach the moment of casting their ballots, it is essential to engage thoughtfully and deliberately in the decision-making process. Supporting a candidate who deviates from conventional expectations can often prove to be a safer and more prudent choice. Why is this the case? Such candidates are more likely to uphold the rule of law and adhere to the principles enshrined in the United States Constitution, along with abiding by established procedures that ensure checks and balances within the government.

Conversely, choosing to back an individual who exhibits clear authoritarian tendencies or displays an insatiable hunger for power raises serious concerns. The looming threat of an unchecked presidency is significant, and the repercussions of embracing such leadership cannot be underestimated. To clarify, what does authoritarianism entail? It refers to a political approach that emphasizes a concentration of power within a single leader or a select elite, minimizing accountability to the populace as outlined in constitutional frameworks. This is the perfect example of authoritarianism, which means favoring a concentration of power in a leader and an elite not constitutionally responsible to the people—to make it simpler, a dictator. Once again, Donald Trump has ordered a four-mile-long military parade on his 79th birthday. This is not Independence Day, it's not Veteran's Day, and it's certainly not a wartime victory celebration. It's Trump's birthday, and on that day, not necessarily for but on that day, he wants tanks and fighter jets and soldiers marching past. That sounds like something out of North Korea or a bad 20th-century flashback to authoritarians/dictators around the world. The date he picked, June 14th, happens to also be the 250th anniversary of the US Army—convenient excuse, right? But make no mistake, because everything for Trump is about Donald Trump. If you're going to have a parade out in the clear blue, why not have it for our veterans who died and fought for this country? He doesn't give a damn about America or veterans.

Let's talk money. Remember when Donald Trump promised to balance the budget during his first term? Not only did that not happen, but now he is back, demanding taxpayer money for what is essentially the vanity project of no real substance. Military parades are very expensive; the last time he tried this, the price tag was estimated at $92 million before it was scrapped. You might wonder how is it so expensive. It turns out that mobilizing all of this military equipment, including preparing the road surfaces on which the road-based elements will move as well as gasoline and fuel of different kinds, is all insanely expensive, and the eventual sort of pared-down salute to America back in 2019 cost twice as much as a typical July 4th celebration, and that didn't even include tanks tearing up the DC streets and the cost to repair those streets. Now in the background of all this, we have the question about its legality, but we also have to remember there were some who said, I think Trump is going to pare down/reduce military spending in conjunction. With the request for this parade, we see that Donald Trump is now moving forward on the biggest military budget in American history, not exactly paring/cutting down military spending.

Ignoring the lessons learned from history could lead the nation down a perilous path toward authoritarianism. This path poses a danger to the very fabric of democracy, where established norms and values begin to erode, and the foundational principles of effective governance are jeopardized. Therefore, it is imperative for citizens to remain vigilant, informed, and engaged in order to protect and preserve the democratic processes that continue to exist.

In the year 2025, the United States finds itself in a troubling situation where democratic principles appear to be eroding. The President is actively attempting to undermine the Constitution. How is that possible?

Undermining the Constitution by attempting to bypass or override its principles could include ignoring the system of checks and balances by overstepping executive powers, refusing to enforce laws passed by Congress, or undermining judicial authority. Another way is by attempting to restrict freedoms guaranteed by the Bill of Rights, like freedom of speech or the press, but remember there are constitutional safeguards in place to prevent such actions from succeeding long term, like congressional oversight and the judicial branch's power to strike down unconstitutional actions, so it's not something easily done or without consequence.

Let's look at a few specific scenarios.

A president might undermine the Constitution by attempting to issue executive orders that violate constitutional limits or infringe on rights like freedom of speech. defy court orders and ignore judicial rulings undermining the judiciary's role in interpreting the law utilize federal agencies to intimidate political opponents or suppress dissent, compromising civil liberties manipulate electoral processes by undermining the integrity of elections or disregarding the peaceful transfer of power. It is a complex issue, but those are some of the ways a president could potentially challenge constitutional norms. The resilience of the Constitution depends on the willingness of other branches of government and the public to uphold it. Just which has long served as the bedrock of American democracy and individual rights.

This alarming move threatens not only the foundational legal framework of the country but also the various protections that ensure the well-being of its citizens. Let's be clear about what democracy is: a form of government in which the people vote directly against or in favor of decisions, policies, and laws. Free and fair elections are a hallmark of American democracy.

Additionally, the administration is systematically cutting essential programs that provide support and resources to those in needs, leaving many Americans vulnerable and without the assistance necessary for a stable life. The implications of these actions are profound, as they compromise the values of justice, equality, and liberty that have defined the nation for centuries. Letting the richest man in the world violate all American privacy. This individual lacks any form of security clearance and has not undergone any verification process or received confirmation regarding their credentials or background.

As a result, their access to sensitive information or secure environments is not authorized. With a corrupt mind and unprecedented power, the world's richest man roams free, wielding his influence to undermine the lives of the poor and warp the fabric of American life.

Congress vows to be a puppet to his whims as a felon and con man dismantles justice. He purges civil servants, inspector generals, and prosecutors, leaving a void where the rule of law once stood. The Republican president becomes an autocrat, signing an executive order granting him and his attorney general the sole authority to interpret the law. Silence falls over Republican congressmen complicit in their muteness. With ruthless efficiency, he slashes through opposition, his bigotry exposed for all to see.

Both of these men are ripping off Americans. How? Cutting government contracts from others and keeping his government contract active, Musk is getting 8 million dollars a day, which is unfair. This blatant favoritism showcases the systemic corruption and cronyism that plague the current administration. The concentration of wealth and power in the hands of a few is eroding the principles of fairness and justice that the nation was founded upon.

The narrative of America is one marked by resilience and reform, showcasing the nation's ability to adapt and grow through challenges and changes over time. Since its founding, the

United States has faced numerous trials, such as wars, economic upheavals, and social movements that sought to redefine justice and equality. Each chapter in this story underscores a collective spirit—individuals and communities rising to meet adversity with determination and innovation.

The pursuit of reform has been a central theme, fueling critical shifts in policies and societal norms driven by a commitment to a more inclusive democracy. Whether through the abolition of slavery, the civil rights movement, or contemporary struggles for justice, the American spirit has consistently embraced the ideals of progress and equity.

This ongoing journey reflects not only the complexities of American identity but also the enduring hope for a better future. The narrative of America is one marked by resilience and reform, showcasing the nation's ability to adapt and grow through challenges and changes over time. Since its founding, the United States has faced numerous trials, such as wars, economic upheavals, and social movements that sought to redefine justice and equality.

The challenges of today demand an unprecedented level of unity and action. It is not enough to merely criticize; we must mobilize and work toward restoring the integrity of our democratic institutions. Let us hold those accountable who betray the public trust and strive to create a society where every individual has the opportunity to thrive.

In conclusion, "America Not So Beautiful" is a clarion call to action. It is a reminder that the fight for a just and equitable society is ongoing and that each of us has a role to

play in shaping the future of this great nation. Now is the time to stand together, resist injustice, and work tirelessly to build a better America for all.

Regarding the president's bigotry, it is all in the open, and quite obviously, he gave the order to terminate certain people. The president claims that immigrants are taking Black jobs from blacks; those were his words. The president's first act. He fired Air Force Black 4-star General CQ Brown, the highest-ranking Black person in the military; the president replaced him with a lower-ranked white person for the position, but the president didn't stop there. He also fired Gwynne Wilcox, the chair of the National Labor Relations Board, who was the first Black woman board member. The president also replaced Lloyd Austin, the Black Secretary of Defense, with an unqualified white Fox News host. The president replaced Michael Regan, the Black EPA Administrator, with an anti-environmental white guy who immediately ended the EPA's Justice program that funded Black communities.

In the education department, where 30% of employees were Black, 64 of the 74 workers who were let go were Black. At the Department of Health and Human Services, 1300 people, 20% of whom were Black, were laid off. In the Department of Veterans Affairs, which lost 1,000 employees, 24% were Black. The president's officials are not hiding their racist motive against Black people. The president's officials said white men must be in charge of everything if you want things to work.

When Truman desegregated the armed forces in 1948 and President Kennedy and President Johnson banned racial discrimination in the federal workforce in the 1960s, the military and the federal government were the few places where Black people could get a good job in the era of racial discrimination. That's why Black people make up 13.7% of the US population but account for nearly 19% of federal workers, and that's why Washington, DC, which used to be called Chocolate City before taking precautions, once had the highest median income for Black people of any city in the country.

Trump rescinded the anti-discrimination rules that had been in place since the 1960s so they could fire Black people at will. We are witnessing the most sweeping presidential attack on Black workers since Woodrow Wilson segregated the federal workforce in 1913. Adam Sandler at The Atlantic calls it the great resegregation.

The reason why Trump is attacking the federal workforce is precisely because it is often more meritocratic and, therefore, more integrated than the private sector, says Server. To get a job in the federal civil service, you have to meet the posted qualifications, including the private sector. According to political terms, a lot of people get jobs through their social networks, according to political scientists. Ashley Jardine says Trump purposely misuses Ashley Jardina. Trump purposely misuses DEI as a synonym for unqualified directly, but he hires the most unqualified white people around the canyon. I don't think it'll wash my hands for 10 years of transportation and education, and they take tests, and the other unqualified boys rummage through your personal information in government databases.

Donald Trump is a felon; he is the first felon to give the State of the Union address in Washington, DC. Donald Trump vowed to be a dictator on his first day in office; he has succeeded in doing just that. He nominated all yes personnel to do his will for retribution. FBI Director, he vowed to do Trump's will by investigating those who brought Trump to trial and other matters. The FBI director says the president is the law. T

rump nominated others who are unqualified and do his will. US Attorney for the United States, the Secretary of Defense, a drunk TV host with no experience whatsoever. He pledges to carry out Trump's wishes. Trump is leading the country in the wrong direction; he has imposed tariffs on Mexico, Canada and China, and then he reversed his decision, and then he put it on pause for 30 days. Trump has no clue what is going on. He also made a statement during his State of the Union: he said Greenland and Canada will belong to the United States one way or another. Trump is willing to force the issue.

In addition, he plans to take over the Gaza Strip and send millions of families and people away from their homes. This is truly not the American way. Trump is a dictator at his heart. Americans need to set aside their differences and stop this madness; they must put the country first.

A madman brought Trump, and he donated millions to his election. Now, he owns Trump. Anything Musk wants done, Trump lets it happen. Musk went on a rampage, cutting government contracts from different people. Stopping them on the spot, but on the other hand, Musk was just awarded a government contract for his pet project for millions, close to billions. The Republican Congress did not say a word about Musk heading for Social Security, Medicare, and Medicaid to cut those programs. After that, he is headed for the Veterans Administration to terminate thousands of veterans. Trump just smiled and got closer to Putin (Russia).

Musk is a menace. Musk wields unprecedented influence over the administration, bypassing traditional checks and balances. His lack of official confirmation or security clearance underscores the alarming erosion of democratic safeguards. The concentration of power in his hands, coupled with his immense wealth, has rendered him a shadow ruler, manipulating the nation's policies to serve his interests. As the richest man in the world, Musk's financial clout has purchased unparalleled access and control, making him a de facto power behind the throne.

Trump's allegiance to Musk has further compromised the integrity of the presidency, turning the highest office in the land into a mere extension of Musk's corporate empire. This unholy alliance has allowed Musk to operate with impunity, disregarding the rule of law and undermining the principles of fairness and justice. The ramifications of this unchecked power are far-reaching, threatening the very foundation of American democracy.

In the face of this unprecedented crisis, the American people must recognize the gravity of the situation and take a stand against the corporate takeover of their government. The fight for a just and equitable society requires vigilance, unity, and a commitment to holding those in power accountable. Only through collective action can the nation hope to reclaim its democratic ideals and ensure a brighter future for all its citizens.

How Trump plans to accomplish this takeover of Canada by using tariffs to pressure them, maybe putting on 250%. The imposition of tariffs on Canada by the Trump administration will undoubtedly cause significant hardship to the country. These tariffs will strain the economic ties between the two nations, leading to increased costs for Canadian businesses and consumers. The agricultural, manufacturing, and automotive sectors, which heavily rely on cross-border trade, will face severe disruptions, resulting in job losses and reduced economic growth.

Moreover, the tariffs will exacerbate the cost of living for ordinary Canadians, as the prices of imported goods rise. Small businesses, in particular, will struggle to absorb the increased costs, leading to potential closures and further unemployment. The ripple effect of these tariffs will be felt across various industries, causing a downturn in the Canadian economy and straining the long-standing friendship between the two countries.

Despite this economic turmoil, the Canadian government and its people must find ways to adapt and persevere. Strengthening domestic industries, seeking new trade partnerships, and fostering innovation will be crucial steps in mitigating the impact of these tariffs.

The resilience and resourcefulness of Canadians will be tested, but through collective effort and determination, the nation can navigate these challenging times and emerge more robust. Trump is very serious; he is talking more and more, and no one is saying anything about his quest to take over Canada.

Musk is cutting research programs; thousands of people will be fired. Musk is making many mistakes, and people are beginning to notice. Nationwide, people are protesting for scientific causes. Many individuals feel that it is unjust to be terminated, particularly by someone who has not been elected.

It appears that Musk may benefit from additional guidance and planning for himself.

There have been instances where his actions could be perceived as a lack of respect for others. In addition, Musk is paying millions for Trump's advertisements at the present time. Musk is still donating millions to Trump even though Trump has already been elected. In a bold move, Trump invited Elon Musk to his first cabinet meeting, signaling a commitment to innovation and forward-thinking leadership. Musk emerged as the key highlight that captivated everyone's attention. The staff quickly recognized that Musk was clearly in command of the situation; he dominated the conversation, sharing his thoughts and ideas with confidence and authority.

It was surprising to note, however, that despite his prominent role in the discussions, he still lacked any form of security clearance, which raised questions about his access to sensitive information and the implications of his influence. It seems like no one questions it. Many of Trump's staff members are intimidated by him and often hesitate to mention his name or discuss certain topics in his presence. They let him do all the talking and suggestions.

Musk continued to fire people; he was so carried away that he made a serious mistake and fired all the air controllers. Trump didn't say a word at that time. After a while, pressure from one of Trump's cabinet teams was overseeing the air controllers. Trump had to try and find them and rehire them. It was a mess and a grave mistake; however, Trump still let this fool Musk go and fired more people.

During the meeting, Musk got into an argument with the secretary of state because Musk fired some people who were under the secretary of state's office. They argued back and forth, and Trump watched like he was watching a tennis match. He chose to take the initiative and offer his perspective. He figured it was time to jump in and share his thoughts.

Even though he sides with Musk indirectly, lots of the staff are beginning to object to Musk directly. No matter how you slice it, the undeniable truth is that Musk is at the helm! There is no President of the United States, just an old, tired man trying to get as much money out of the government as he can. As Trump said to a governor when he met with all the governors, she said she is going to follow the rule of law and doesn't care what the White House says. Trump said, "I'm the law and the government, and you will comply or you will not get any funding from here." The governor said, "I will see you in court. Trump said, "good, that will be easy because no one will elect you anymore." It's hard to believe a United States president would talk like that.

This president is all out to exercise his power for retribution. He has specifically focused on law firms that took the initiative to investigate his actions and subsequently filed charges against him. This behavior is not only alarming but also represents a severe misuse of power and a disregard for the legal process. It is an outrage that highlights the lengths he will go to in order to retaliate against those seeking justice.

Trump has effectively created an atmosphere of fear and silence, where many individuals feel compelled to keep their criticisms and dissenting opinions to themselves. This pervasive sense of apprehension stems from the intimidation he wields over those who oppose him, leading to a reluctance to speak out or express differing viewpoints. As a result, it seems as though he has put a metaphorical muzzle on anyone who might challenge his authority, fostering an environment where open dialogue and honest discourse are stifled. The individual in the presidency has issued hundreds of executive orders and participated in numerous interviews and public appearances in anticipation of the upcoming midterm elections.

However, throughout all of these engagements, there has been a noticeable absence of any mention regarding strategies to lower prices or address the escalating costs affecting everyday citizens. There has not been a single instance in which the so-called president has discussed collaborating with Congress to tackle these pressing economic issues.

This lack of focus raises questions about the administration's priorities and commitment to addressing the financial challenges faced by the public. His supporters put him in office because they figured Trump was their savior who would fix everything and bring down prices, like gas, food, cars, etc.

Instead, the clown spends more time on his golf course. He keeps forgetting running a business and running a government are very different. You must not run a government like a business; Americans will suffer, so he runs to his golf course like a businessman taking a break. Trump has played on his Florida golf course and has now cost American taxpayers 18 million dollars since he regained the presidency, sitting on the pace to exceed the $151.5 million he spent in his first term.

This weekend, Trump is playing golf for the 13th day of his 48 days in office. It was his 10th day playing another course in West Palm Beach across the Intracoastal Waterway from his Mar-a-Lago country club home and adjacent to the Palm Beach County Jail, where he belongs. This clown is a disgrace. Getting back to Musk, this bastard has informed the social security staff to leave; he said the staff will be paid for a year if they leave now.

Everything Musk said is a lie, saying people are getting the benefit at the age of 150 years old. A lot of dead people are collecting Social Security. The reality is that both Donald Trump and Elon Musk are having a detrimental impact on the social security system. A former Social Security commissioner has voiced concerns that if they continue to influence policy in this manner, the current benefits could potentially face delays of approximately 60 to 90 days. This situation arises from a strategic push to encourage people to exit the system, which may undermine its stability and accessibility for those who rely on these benefits. As a result, the financial security of many individuals could be at risk if these trends persist. This is going to cause a serious protest, even a violent one.

Trump is one of the greatest con men in the world; he has come to his supporters to the extreme. Even though Trump is causing chaos in this country, his supporters are totally blind. In my opinion, Trump wants to take over the world.

The way I see it, he is siding with Russia and turning his back on his allies.

Trump cut off funding for Ukraine. When his secretary of state tried to broach the subject of funding Ukraine, Trump set him aside—in other words, told him to sit down and shut up about the funding. At this point, Trump going back and forth regarding the tariff has created a situation where certain individuals, including him, are finding ways to profit from this particular strategy. This back-and-forth suggests a complex negotiation process, and amidst this uncertainty, some parties are leveraging the fluctuations and implications of the tariff adjustments to their financial advantage. During his campaign, Trump promised his supporters that he would lower prices on his first day in office. After spending 40 days in office, he held a press conference to announce a significant change in economic policy related to tariffs.

He revealed that effective April 2nd, 2025, there would be an increase in prices across various sectors as a direct consequence of the newly implemented tariffs.

During his address, he emphasized that there were no intentions to roll back these tariffs or reduce prices in the foreseeable future. This announcement sparked widespread confusion and concern among consumers, businesses, and economists, who began to question the implications of these tariffs on the overall market stability and the cost of living. The uncertainty surrounding the situation left many wondering how these changes would affect both domestic and international trade relations moving forward. Trump is making it easy for him to seal and do illegal transactions. This is why he fired all the inspector generals; they oversee everything to ensure transactions are legitimate, generally speaking. Anyone who can keep an eye on him and stop him or object to what he is doing, he will fire them.

The Republican-controlled Congress granted him a considerable degree of freedom in his actions and decisions, enabling him to pursue his agenda without significant interference. However, behind closed doors, many members of the party expressed their reservations and concerns regarding his strategies and choices, voicing objections that they preferred to keep out of the public eye. Ethics top watchdog Hampton Dillinger was very serious about his job. Trump fired him out of the blue because he questioned the tariff. Let me share with you who the top 5 countries are and how much they contributed to the United States of America's economy as exporters. #5 Germany $160 billion in goods are exported every year. From sleek BMWs and Mercedes to engineering from sleek precision-engineered machinery and top-notch pharmaceuticals, German engineering excellence truly drives its trade power #4.

Japan delivers a solid $172 billion worth of exports to the US annually, from reliable cars like Toyota and Honda to state-of-the-art electronics. Japan is the go-to partner for technology and innovation, and sliding into 3rd place is Mexico with a jaw-dropping $455 billion in exports thanks to its close proximity. Mexico is the ultimate trade buddy, sending cars, electronics, and even fresh avocados to stock US shelves. #2 China, with a staggering $550 billion in exports, from the smartphones in your pocket to the laptops on your desk China is the backbone of everyday consumer goods in the US and is finally taking the best and finally taking the crown at #1.

Canada, with a mind-blowing $665 billion in exports every year, isn't just your friendly neighbor; it's the backbone of America's economy, from energy that powers cities to vehicles cruising down every highway and timber that builds everything from homes to skyscrapers. Canada's goods are literally shaping the American dream.

Trump is money hungry; it's not "let's work together." No, I want all of it. Trump put in an executive order to sell his coin. This has nothing to do with the economy; it has everything to do with putting money in that clown's pocket. It is sad. The fact of the matter is that he is treating the North American economy as individuals treat the financial markets almost like a personal plaything, as they fluctuate dramatically in response to each presidential election victory.

Donald Trump is anticipated to receive a luxurious Boeing 747 jet from Qatar, a development that has sparked considerable controversy and raised a series of legal and ethical questions. The situation becomes particularly complex given the possibility that the aircraft could serve as the new Air Force One during his presidency and subsequently be transferred to his presidential library after he leaves office.

Qatar's foreign nations' involvement adds another layer to the debate, especially since the U.S. Constitution's foreign emoluments clause explicitly bars government officials from accepting gifts from foreign states without obtaining congressional consent. Article 1, Section 9, Clause 8 of the US Constitution safeguards against conflicts of interest and ensures officials prioritize national interest over personal gain. It's considered an impeachable offense; violating the emoluments clause might be considered a breach of the president's duty to uphold the Constitution. Impeachment is ultimately a political process, so it depends on Congress's interpretation and action. Since Trump owns the Republicans in Congress, I doubt they would do anything, even though it's clearly a bribe, and accepting a gift from a foreign nation shows just how corrupt Congress operates. The Republicans will just turn their heads.

This scenario presents a unique and controversial challenge regarding legality and ethics.

While Qatar is generally regarded as a friendly nation with which the United States has formed a strategic partnership—particularly in areas of defense, security, and economic cooperation the crux of the issue lies not in the diplomatic relations between the two countries but rather in the potential ramifications of a high-value gift from a foreign government.

Critics argue that Trump's acceptance of such a substantial gift, valued at approximately half a billion dollars, contravenes constitutional provisions meant to safeguard against foreign influence in American politics. Many are observing the silence from Republican lawmakers regarding this matter, raising concerns about the integrity of the 118th Congress in 2025.

There is a palpable sense of outrage that suggests had this situation involved former Presidents Obama or Biden, the response from congressional Republicans would have been swift and severe—likely resulting in calls for impeachment articles. Let's be clear, I am not with either party, Democrat or Republican, I believe in what is right and what is wrong, I fought for my Country—this Country is going down the toilet because of Trump's incompetence and greed and this so-called President is against the rule of law 100%.

Many see Trump as driven by a voracious hunger for money and power, labeling him the most corrupt and ineffective president in the history of the United States. This situation underscores the ongoing debate about ethics in political office and the extent to which foreign influence can infiltrate domestic governance.

This constant shifting reflects the way political outcomes can significantly influence economic sentiment, investor behavior, and trading strategies, with the markets reacting to every win and loss. I will try to break down what Trump is doing regarding the tariff situation.

Donald Trump is lying to you. Here's the truth: it's simple. Tariffs are attacks on Americans. When you buy something, you pay the tariff, not some foreign country. Trump's tariffs will raise the price of things like tomatoes and prescription medicines. Electronics, toys, and grocery prices are rising because of Trump's tax. New car prices are rising because of Trump's tax. Beer prices are rising because of Trump's tax, and he has no plan for what happens next. He doesn't care about the farmer, the farm, or the small business that depends significantly on specialized machinery sourced from Canada to ensure its operations run smoothly and efficiently.

This equipment plays a crucial role in various tasks, from planting and harvesting crops to facilitating daily business activities. The reliability and advanced technology of Canadian machinery contribute to enhancing productivity and maintaining high standards within the operation. An owner who needs supplies from Europe or the parents who need to feed their families every day at a reasonable cost.

Regarding the deficit, Republicans voted to reduce government spending. However, under the current trajectory of Trump's policies, it appears that expectations may not be met. If the Republican plan is implemented, even under the most optimistic assumptions—which are not entirely accurate—there will be an addition of $300 billion to the deficit this year, $295 billion the following year, and $242 billion in subsequent years. Trump is out of control, and the Republicans are letting this happen.

Why?

Trump wants loyalty. Donald Trump has made it very clear that he wants people who are loyal to him personally and not to the office or to the Constitution, and that's a deep concern when you look at Trump's agenda. It really suggests a politicization of the nonpartisan leadership of America's armed forces if generals are being replaced based on perceived political loyalty to the president, and I think to remember again that U.S. Congress has a role in this.

The Senate has to confirm Trump's new chairman of the Joint Chiefs, and I think it's an appropriate set of questions for them to ask as to why this apparently retired general has been elevated to this position and what questions were asked of him by Donald Trump. This clown is so corrupt and unreal.

Trump is threatening Iran, which means Russia is going to come to play. Russia is allied to Iran. The stock market has experienced a significant decline, plummeting by more than 1,000 points, a direct consequence of the tariffs imposed by President Trump. This economic downturn has raised concerns among analysts and citizens alike, yet President Trump remains steadfast in his denial of the existence of a recession.

Compounding the situation, Russia is persisting with its military aggression against Ukraine, further destabilizing the region. In response to the ongoing conflict, the Secretary of State is actively engaging in diplomatic efforts and is currently in meetings with Saudi Arabian officials, focusing on peace negotiations aimed at addressing the crisis in Ukraine and fostering stability in the area. Trump has other ideas. Let me take you to approximately two weeks ago; you will be able to see what Trump's motive is. top American and Ukrainian officials who made us Saudi Arabia for a series of high-stakes talks about the ongoing war with Russia This will be the first meeting since the absolute train wreck in the Oval Office when Donald Trump and JD Vance bullied and berated President Zelensky, and somehow things have only gone downhill over the past few days. Trump paused both military aid and intelligence assistance to Ukraine, and Russia took full advantage, launching devastating, deadly strikes on Ukrainian troops and supply lines so the Ukrainians clearly need this aid, and now Trump is making it even harder to get it back.

Trump had been pursuing a mineral deal with Ukraine, as we all know, as a condition to restore aid, but as NBC News reported this weekend, Trump has privately made clear that the Assad mineral deal won't be enough to restart aid and intelligence sharing, so the question now is if the mineral deal isn't enough, according to NBC.

Trump also wants to see a change in presence unless his attitude toward peace talks includes a willingness to make concessions, such as giving up territory to Russia. So he wants a concession, a change in attitude, and territorial concessions. By the way, Trump's buddy Vladimir Putin remembers him and certainly wants this. Well, there's got to be more, right? Well, as NBC News reports, Trump also wants to make some movement. Just a little movement towards elections in Ukraine and possibly Zelensky stepping down as his country's leader, and there it is—that's the end game, and that sounds an awful lot like what the problem, the Kremlin, has been saying and wanting for years.

Russia's top diplomat says Russia wants to get rid of Zelensky. That's a blunt admission and a devastating warning: Russia aims to topple Zelensky and his government. The foreign minister says the Kremlin's goal has been clear for a very, very long time: remove Zelensky and install a puppet regime in his place. For you people wondering what's wrong with President Volodymyr Zelensky, the leader of Ukraine, is a strong advocate for democracy, human rights, and the fair treatment of all individuals. He believes in upholding these values not only for Ukrainians but also for people around the world. In contrast, the actions of Russia under President Vladimir Putin stand in stark opposition to these ideals.

The relationship between the United States and Ukraine has been complex, particularly in the context of Russian aggression. While the U.S. has historically supported Ukraine, there have been periods of tension, especially during the Trump administration. Trump has turned his back on Ukraine and taken sides with Putin. Some Republican leaders appeared to question the level of support provided to Ukraine in its conflict with Russia.

However, the Republican Congress still does whatever Trump tells them to do. Putin's regime has often resorted to extreme measures to suppress dissent and eliminate opponents. These tactics can include political assassinations, rigged elections, and other forms of intimidation, all of which serve to undermine democracy. Unlike Zelensky's vision for Ukraine, which embraces democratic principles and human rights, the Russian government continues to operate in a manner that dismisses these values entirely, contributing to ongoing instability in the region.

As the international community looks on, the conflict between Ukraine and Russia highlights not just a territorial dispute but a deeper struggle between democratic governance and authoritarian rule. Trump, in my opinion, is a con man and very good at what he does. In the election of 2025, he emerged victorious, yet astonishingly, he openly declared that the entire electoral process was rigged. <u>I have a RECORDED VIDEO of him making that statement.</u> His claims seemed to reflect a deep-seated confidence, as if he were fully aware that his supporters would overlook the contradiction in his statement.

This audacity showcases his remarkable skill as a con man, knowing that, regardless of the controversy, many would choose to ignore the implications of his words and believe in his narrative. It is as if he operates under the assumption that the truth doesn't matter as long as he maintains his grip on his audience. I believe it. Before he was elected to a term, he had classified documents that were in his possession and were shared with various individuals, each of whom had a specific interest or need for the information maybe contained within them. He took great care in selecting whom to share these documents with, ensuring that those receiving them would derive value or insight from the contents.

The evidence presented in the recorded footage showcased a compelling case against former President Trump, leading to serious legal repercussions. He was found guilty of election interference, a charge that raised significant concerns about the integrity of the democratic process. Furthermore, he was also convicted of rape, a serious crime that underscores past allegations against him.

Despite these serious convictions, his staunch supporters, often referred to as MAGA supporters, continue to fervently back him. They seem largely unconcerned with the implications of these legal judgments, demonstrating a loyalty that some find perplexing. In contrast, many believe that if anyone else had faced the same allegations and convictions, they would have been subjected to far harsher repercussions, highlighting a perceived double standard in the treatment of public figures in the political arena.

The Republican Party was behind him. They nominated him for president. It was a sad moment in history that a convicted rapist was making headlines as he was set to be in the White House during his second term in office. This unprecedented situation raised numerous questions and sparked widespread outrage among the public and advocacy groups. Many wondered how a person with such a serious criminal history could gain access to the nation's highest political institution, prompting discussions about security, morality, and the implications for victims of sexual violence.

Throughout his presidency, he issued over 500 executive orders, reflecting a significant and nontraditional approach to governance. His agenda diverged dramatically from the norms typically seen in previous administrations, prioritizing bold and sometimes controversial initiatives that aimed to reshape key policies across various sectors. Nominated in many instances, we encounter individuals who, despite their lack of qualifications or experience, find themselves in positions of significant responsibility and influence. This phenomenon raises important questions about the criteria used for selecting leaders and decision-makers in vital sectors.

It is essential to examine the implications of placing such unqualified individuals in critical roles, as their decisions can significantly impact outcomes and the effectiveness of various strategies can be illustrated through specific examples, such as those found within the Department of Defense. In this context, examining how the department implements policies and measures can provide valuable insights into its operational success and areas for improvement.

For example, he was a drunk and a womanizer, plus the head of the CIA and the head of the FBI, Homeland Security was unqualified, and many more. All of the individuals in question lacked the necessary qualifications for their positions.

However, despite their deficiencies, they were unwavering, loyal supporters of Trump. This loyalty often influenced their actions and decisions, prioritizing allegiance over expertise. In his pursuit of vengeance against those who had wronged him, he surrounded himself with a group of loyal followers. However, to his dismay, he realized that they were nothing more than a collection of yes-men, always eager to agree with him without offering any real insight or challenge to his plans. Their unwavering support left him isolated in his single-minded quest, lacking the diverse perspectives that could have guided him to a more strategic approach.

The Republican Senate didn't care; they confirmed each person because Trump wanted them, and they didn't care Trump used his power for revenge. Musk is out of control, closing the public, growing increasingly discontent with Elon Musk's recent decisions, took matters into their own hands and began to express their frustration in tangible ways. This backlash reached a peak when some individuals resorted to vandalizing his car business, a clear sign of their anger and disappointment. As a consequence of these actions and his controversial choices—such as cutting vital programs and making significant changes to Social Security—Musk experienced substantial financial losses, totaling billions of dollars.

Amidst this turmoil, President Donald Trump sensed an opportunity to intervene. He recognized the mounting frustrations among the voter base and decided to address the situation. Trump's next steps were crucial in shaping his political narrative and garnering support from his party and those affected by these developments. He asked the Republican Party to step in to support Elon Musk as he navigates through significant financial losses. This support comes amid growing concerns about the impact of these losses on his various ventures. President Trump has also expressed his backing for Musk, highlighting the importance of his contributions to innovation and the economy. Let Elon Musk arrange for several of his electric cars to be displayed prominently on the White House lawn, creating quite a spectacle. Meanwhile, President Donald Trump took to social media to promote the initiative, praising the innovative technology and highlighting its significance for American industry and environmental sustainability.

The notion of conducting business within the White House has historically been quite uncommon and even controversial. However, during Donald Trump's presidency, this practice became more prominent, leading to numerous discussions and debates about its implications and ethics.

In a surprising turn of events, President Donald Trump purchased a high-end vehicle from Elon Musk, the CEO of Tesla. This transaction drew significant public attention due to the stature of both individuals and the implications it might have in the realm of politics and business. Moreover, during a recent public address, Trump went on to suggest if protesting in front of the Musk car dealership, he might pursue legislation defining certain actions as domestic terrorism. This bold statement sparked widespread debate about how such a law could impact civil liberties and the political landscape in the United States.

Trump is working on, in my view, we are experiencing a kind of internal conflict that resembles a civil war. It seems that he is attempting to dismantle or eliminate certain established systems or principles that many people hold dear. For instance, our civil rights This effort reflects a deeper struggle within our society, highlighting the divisions and challenges we face as we navigate through these turbulent times.

Moreover, he weaponized the Department of Justice. There have been claims regarding the Department of Justice under the current administration. Reports suggest that the US attorney appointed by Trump may prosecute individuals who oppose him, according to certain articles. The trade war between the United States and Canada is intensifying, with Canada showing no signs of backing down on the issue of tariffs. In response to recent U.S. tariffs, the Canadian government has decided to implement additional tariffs on a range of American goods, aiming to protect its domestic industries.

In a significant escalation, President Trump announced a staggering 200% tariff on Canadian wine and alcoholic beverages, which has raised concerns about the potential ramifications for businesses and consumers on both sides of the border. This erratic approach to trade policy is creating considerable chaos within the United States, as the president frequently shifts his stance, leading to heightened uncertainty in the market.

Remarkably, it has been less than 60 days since Trump took office, yet his administration's unpredictable actions have already led to significant tensions in the U.S.-Canada relationship, leaving many to wonder how this ongoing trade war will unfold in the coming months.

President Trump is currently awaiting a response from Russia regarding the proposed ceasefire agreement. While Ukraine has already expressed its willingness to accept the terms of the ceasefire, the pivotal factor now lies in whether President Putin will agree to the proposal. Trump's decision-making process hinges on this outcome, as he closely monitors the situation to gauge Russia's stance and the potential implications of the ongoing conflict.

On March 13, 2025, a pivotal moment is set to unfold in Washington, D.C., as the Senate prepares for a crucial vote regarding a government-funding bill that was recently passed by the House of Representatives. The stakes are high, as a successful vote is essential to avoid a government shutdown. Republican leaders, including President Trump, have urged all party members to unify in support of the bill, emphasizing the need for a solid Republican front.

The bill has drawn significant controversy, particularly among Democratic senators who are strategically poised to oppose it. Their hope lies in swaying enough votes to prevent the bill from passing, thus allowing the government to close down. Some Democrats argue that the bill's provisions lack the necessary bipartisan support and address issues they deem nonpartisan and detrimental to public welfare.

As the clock ticks down to the final vote scheduled for March 14, 2025, both parties are bracing for a political showdown. Democrats remain optimistic that they can rally sufficient opposition to prevent passage, while Republicans are working diligently to consolidate their votes. It's a high-stakes scenario, leaving everyone to wonder if the political landscape will shift in the final hours. Leading up to the vote, potentially swaying more Democrats to join their Republican counterparts in favor of the bill. The outcome remains uncertain as both sides gear up for what could be a decisive moment in the ongoing budgetary stalemate.

In a surprising turn of events, President Donald Trump and his associate Elon Musk initiated significant workforce reductions across various federal agencies, including the State Department, the Department of Veterans Affairs, the Internal Revenue Service, and the Federal Aviation Administration. This aggressive action resulted in the dismissal of thousands of employees, sparking widespread concern and outrage among public sector workers and unions.

In response to these mass firings, numerous lawsuits were filed by the affected employees, claiming unlawful termination and violations of their rights. These legal challenges quickly gained momentum, as many employees rallied together to seek justice.

After approximately two months of legal battles, the court system ultimately ruled in favor of the employees. The judges ordered that all terminated federal workers be reinstated to their previous positions. Furthermore, the court mandated that these individuals would receive back pay for the duration of their unemployment, effectively ensuring they would be compensated for their lost wages during the dispute.

As the situation unfolds, stakeholders are closely monitoring the developments. Employees are preparing to return to their jobs, while legal experts and government officials assess the implications of these rulings on future employment practices within federal agencies. The outcome could significantly impact how employee terminations are handled moving forward. In revisiting the topic of President Trump's foreign policy, it has become increasingly evident how his administration's actions have strained relations with traditional American allies. A recent report highlighted that Portugal has opted to cancel its order for F-35 fighter jets from the United States. Instead, the country plans to modernize its military by replacing its aging F-16 fleet with European-made aircraft. This decision underscores a growing uncertainty among our allies regarding America's reliability as a defense partner.

The broader implications of this shift are concerning. The predictability and strength of alliances that we once counted on are now in jeopardy, leading to a national security landscape that feels less stable. Observers argue that Trump's foreign policy approaches, particularly in relation to Russia, have diminished the United States' standing on the global stage. Some critics even suggest that these actions have transformed America into a pariah state, seemingly to curry favor with Russian President Vladimir Putin. This development raises significant questions about the future of NATO and other crucial alliances formed over decades.

President Trump is addressing the Panama Canal issue. The White House has instructed the US military to create options for reclaiming the Panama Canal, which the United States handed over to Panama more than 25 years ago.

The Panama Canal, a key maritime route connecting the Atlantic and Pacific Oceans, was controlled by the United States until December 31 , 1999, when control was transferred to

Panama under the terms of the Torrijos-Carter Treaties signed in 1977. This strategic waterway has been vital for international trade and military operations, allowing ships to bypass the lengthy and hazardous journey around the southern tip of South America.

This effort aims to deter China, as there are concerns that China might try to control parts of the canal and prevent US ships from using it in case of a conflict. The Chinese government has been increasingly investing in infrastructure projects worldwide, including ports and canals, raising alarms about their growing influence in global transportation networks. Such control could significantly impact both supplies and the US military, potentially disrupting trade routes and hampering the logistical capabilities of the United States armed forces during critical times.

In response to these geopolitical concerns, various strategies are being considered, ranging from diplomatic efforts to renegotiate treaties with Panama to potential military interventions aimed at securing the canal. The situation underscores the importance of maintaining access to crucial maritime passages and protecting national interests in the face of emerging global powers.

In a dramatic turn of events, President Donald Trump recently called a press conference to announce his latest approach to his retribution plan. The setting for this announcement was none other than the Department of Justice, a move that has sparked significant controversy and debate.

President Trump's choice of location for his speech raised immediate concerns. Traditionally, the Department of Justice operates independently from the executive branch to ensure impartiality and uphold the rule of law. By speaking from the Department of Justice, Trump blurred the lines of separation between the executive branch and the judicial system, igniting a firestorm of criticism.

During his speech, Trump outlined his approach to his retribution plan. He made it clear that he intended to use the full force of the Department of Justice to carry out his agenda. This included aggressive actions against his political adversaries, a move that many viewed as an abuse of power and an affront to democratic principles. Adding to the controversy, the US Attorney General was scheduled to speak and share her vision for the future of the Department of Justice. However, Trump's rhetoric suggested that the Attorney General would be acting under his direct orders, further eroding the perceived independence of the Justice Department.

This situation has raised profound questions about the constitutional integrity of the United States' governance system. The executive branch is designed to be separate from the judicial branch to prevent abuses of power. By referring to the Department of Justice as "his department of Justice" and asserting his control over the US Attorney General, Trump has been accused of undermining this crucial separation.

The Democratic Party responded with outrage. Leading figures within the party condemned Trump's actions as unconstitutional and corrupt. They argued that using the Justice Department as a tool for political retribution sets a dangerous precedent and threatens the very foundations of American democracy.

The fallout from Trump's press conference is likely to have lasting political repercussions. Legal experts and constitutional scholars are weighing in on the potential implications, while public opinion is sharply divided.

The incident has intensified the already polarized political climate, with supporters and detractors of Trump clashing over the legitimacy and ethics of his actions.

As the situation unfolds, all eyes are on the Department of Justice and the US Attorney General. Will they comply with Trump's directives, or will they assert their independence and uphold the rule of law? The coming days and eeks will be critical in determining the future of the Justice Department and its role within the broader framework of American governance.

The controversy surrounding Trump's press conference underscores the importance of maintaining the separation of powers and safeguarding democratic institutions. It serves as a stark reminder of the delicate balance that must be preserved to ensure that the rule of law prevails and that no single branch of government becomes too powerful.

Ultimately, the resolution of this issue will have far-reaching implications for the integrity of the United States' constitutional system and the preservation of its democratic values.

In a troubling incident involving the Department of Justice, a high-ranking attorney found herself embroiled in a complex case that garnered significant attention. The case concerned a well-known celebrity, a prominent figure with a vast following, who had lost his right to possess firearms due to a documented history of domestic violence. This incident not only had legal ramifications but also highlighted the severe consequences that arise from such behaviors, particularly in the context of firearm regulations.

The attorney, a dedicated employee working directly under the US Attorney General, was responsible for reviewing the application for the reinstatement of the celebrity's gun privileges.

As part of the process, she meticulously assessed the case, weighing the legal implications and the celebrity's past actions. In accordance with the established procedures, she prepared her recommendation, suggesting that the celebrity should not be granted the right to reinstate his firearm privileges due to his domestic violence record.

Upon completing her review, the attorney received an email from the Deputy Attorney General, giving the green light for the reinstatement. However, the weight of this decision weighed heavily on her conscience. Filled with doubt and concern for the integrity of the justice system, she lay awake at night, reconsidering the implications of her actions. The following day, she approached the Deputy Attorney General seeking clarification on the decision to reinstate such permissions. In response, the Deputy Attorney General dismissed her concerns, insisting that she simply follow protocol and assuring her that everything would be fine.

Despite the pressure, the attorney remained resolute in her belief that personal conduct, particularly regarding domestic violence, should not be overlooked, especially when it came to firearm possession. She decided to adhere to the rule of law, firmly stating that due to his domestic violence history, the celebrity should be denied reinstatement of his gun rights.

Later that day, she received an unexpected phone call from the US Attorney General, who had been appointed by President Trump. The tone of the conversation was alarming; the Attorney General explicitly instructed her to proceed with the reinstatement of the celebrity's gun privileges, framing the directive within the context of the celebrity's friendship with the President.

The Attorney General's message was clear: disregarding the President's wishes would lead to serious consequences. Faced with an ethical dilemma, the attorney stood her ground and refused to follow the order. The very next day, she was terminated from her position, receiving a stark reminder from the US Attorney General that those who oppose the directives associated with the President would face dire repercussions. This incident exemplified not only the intricate intersection of personal relationships and legal authority but also the troubling reality of how political pressure can influence critical legal decisions.

During a recent speech at the Department of Justice (DOJ), President Donald Trump intensified his onslaught against the rule of law by targeting his critics and the judiciary. In his remarks, he asserted that criticizing a judge is illegal, a claim that runs contrary to the First Amendment rights enshrined in the U.S. Constitution, which guarantees freedom of speech.

Furthermore, Trump directed the DOJ to investigate and take action against specific law firms involved in the prosecution of his cases. This directive has raised significant concerns among legal experts and commentators, who argue that such moves undermine the independence of the judiciary and the principle of fair trial.

In response to Trump's actions, judges have deemed these executive orders unconstitutional, affirming that the attempts to pursue law firms involved in the legal proceedings against him lack legitimate grounding.

Critics emphasize that this behavior is not only an affront to established legal norms but also presents a threat to the integrity of the legal system as a whole.

Trump is very prejudiced and doesn't hide it. He fired or gave instructions to fire top military leaders who were Black as well as top leaders in different programs high up in the government who were Black. This man is power-struck and power-hungry.

When Trump was young and trying to get into business, he took out a loan from his father. Trump purchased some apartments to rent. He refused to rent to Black people. Moreover, one reason he didn't want to go into service was that he would be around Black people. He wanted no part of the service; he had his father fix it so the armed forces would not call him. He is a coward, Draff Dodgers. He is also a bully who never apologizes for anything and never accepts any mistakes or errors he makes.

At this present time, the president has ordered strikes on Iran-backed Houthi rebels in Yemen; in addition, he has warned Iran to stop supporting the rebel group. The President promised to use overwhelming lethal force until Iranian-backed Houthi rebels cease their attacks on shipping along the maritime corridor. It's okay to protect the United States from being attacked. If the president starts to attack Houthi rebels, Iran will have something to say, and if Trump tries to attack Iran for any reason, he will have to deal with Russia because Russia is Iran's ally and close partner, Serbia. Trump is so power-struck that he doesn't think. We don't want World War III.

Trump turned his back on most of America's allies. The Republican Congress let him do whatever he wanted. Speaking about World War 3, Trump is always bringing that up. In March 2025, Trump warned that World War III could very easily erupt if peace talks between Russia and Ukraine fail. He was speaking at the

Justice Department. He described the potential conflict as a war like no other due to nuclear weapons. Trump said this could lead to World War 3 very easily, the United States president said. He added that such a conflict would be devastating because of nuclear weapons and other types of weapons that you don't want to know about. Trump claimed the situation was now in pretty good shape compared to before his involvement. It is very frightening because he speaks like it's nothing. I've never heard a US president talk in that manner. It is unreal how he started in politics.

Before Donald Trump's political career, Donald Trump was a prominent real estate developer and businessman. He inherited a real estate company from his father, which he expanded significantly, developing high-profile properties in Manhattan, for instance, the Trump Tower. He also ventured into various businesses. Donald Trump was born in 1946 in Queens, NY. He was a businessman and television personality. He took control of his family's real estate business in 1971, renaming it the Trump Organization. Throughout the 80s and 90s, Trump expanded his empire, building casinos, hotels, and golf courses.

In 2004, he became a household name as the host of the reality TV show The Apprentice. The combination of real estate ventures and media presence set the stage for his entry into politics. After making a name for himself in business and television, Trump began to publicly express political ambitions in the late 1980s. He made his first presidential run in 2000 as a Reform Party candidate but withdrew before voting began.

In 2015, Trump announced his candidacy for the presidency as a Republican. His campaign, marked by controversial statements and policies, resonated with many voters. He won the Republican nomination and then the presidency in the 2016 election, serving as the 45th president of the United States from 2017 to 2021. As a Republican, his policies focus on immigration and trade and promise to make America great again despite numerous controversies, also implementing various policies on taxes and foreign affairs.

His presidency was characterized by a highly polarized political climate after his presidency. Donald Trump remained influential in the Republican Party. He faced an unprecedented 2nd impeachment by the House of Representatives in January 2021 related to the Capitol riot. He was acquitted by the Senate. He has hinted at the possibility of running for president again in future elections and continues to be a polarized figure in American politics after leaving the presidency in January 2021. Trump remained active in politics. Recently, he signed a flurry of executive orders, including repealing several of Joe Biden's policies, initiating an immigration crackdown, and withdrawing the US from the Paris Climate Accord. He also pardoned individuals involved in the January 6th Capitol attack. In terms of trade, Trump hinted at imposing tariffs and has taken steps to pause Congress' TikTok ban while seeking a US buyer to protect national security interests. This action continues to spark legal and logistical debates.

In 2022, Donald Trump remained a key political figure; he continued to influence the

Republican Party and was involved in endorsing and campaigning for various candidates during the midterm elections. Trump also faced multiple legal challenges focusing on his business practices and his role in the January 6th Capitol riot. In 2023, Donald Trump continued playing a significant role in the political scene, influencing Republican policies and engaging with his support through rallies and social media. Trump also faced legal scrutiny, particularly regarding his business dealings and involvement in the events of January 6th. Among the issues were investigations into his business practices, focusing on allegations of financial misconduct and tax fraud.

Additionally, Trump would understand me for his role in the January 6th Capitol riot, with investigations examining his involvement in inciting the event leading up to the riot. These legal challenges continue to impact his public profile and political involvement. Currently today, Donald Trump is facing a 54% disapproval rating on economics handling, but the Republican Party is saying the nation is moving in the right direction. Also, he's been involved in swiftly deporting immigrants linked to the Venezuelan gang Tren de Aragua, citing the Alien Enemies Act, an 18th-century law, claiming its members have infiltrated the US and are engaged in hostile action. This move is controversial because it bypasses the standard immigration court process, removing a layer of legal recourse for those targeted. This action bypasses the usual immigration court process, expediting deportation. On the international stage, President Trump's forthcoming conversation with President Putin is of significant importance. The primary focus is on negotiating a ceasefire in Ukraine, which involves delicate discussions about land concessions.

These talks are part of a broader effort to resolve the conflict, carrying high stakes for international relations. This situation is complex, reflecting the tension and intricate negotiations typical of global politics. President Donald Trump remains at the center of controversy as he continues to contest various legal directives on immigration enforcement.

Recently, a court judge issued a formal order aimed at halting deportations conducted by the Immigration and Customs Enforcement (ICE) agency. Despite this judicial mandate, Trump has openly defied the court's ruling, raising questions about the implications of such challenges to the legal system.

Recent reports have unveiled serious allegations concerning the operations of U.S. Immigration and Customs Enforcement (ICE), pointing to potential civil rights violations involving more than 21 American citizens. These allegations arise during the agency's intelligence-gathering activities aimed at deportation, raising significant concerns about the methodologies employed by ICE and the treatment of individuals subject to enforcement actions. The implications of these allegations suggest a troubling pattern of conduct that may infringe upon the rights of citizens, casting a shadow over the agency's legitimacy and practices.

In a related development, a judge has issued a demand for President Donald Trump to comply with existing court orders, expressing strong disapproval of the actions taken by the Department of Justice. This judicial intervention highlights ongoing tensions in the legal landscape surrounding Trump, reinforcing the need for oversight and accountability in matters involving government agencies.

Moreover, Trump's administration is reportedly taking steps to defund critical organizations such as Radio Free Europe/Radio Liberty and the Voice of America, initiatives that many view as crucial for promoting democratic values and providing independent news coverage. Critics interpret these funding cuts as an alarming shift towards authoritarianism, the road to dictatorship, which could undermine U.S. influence on global media platforms and diminish support for the very principles of free expression and democracy that the nation has long championed.

The ramifications of these actions could have lasting effects on both domestic policy and international relations, as the United States navigates its role in an increasingly complex global landscape.

Donald Trump is engaging in a deliberate campaign to undermine the foundational structures of the U.S. government, with the end goal of sidestepping the rule of law in order to establish a form of dictatorial control.

One of his first actions has been to revoke the pardons granted by President Joe Biden, signifying a broader agenda to erase any policies or initiatives that he perceives as obstacles to his authority. Rather than addressing the pressing issues faced by everyday Americans, Trump appears focused on consolidating power and dismantling the achievements of his predecessor.

In concert with influential figures like Elon Musk, Trump is effectively orchestrating a takeover of governmental functions, all while Congress seems to stand by in silent complicity. This inaction from legislative representatives raises the troubling prospect that by the time any meaningful response is initiated, it will be too late to restore political norms and accountability.

Moreover, Trump's increasingly concerning mental health has become a topic of discussion among some observers, yet it remains largely overlooked by those in positions of power who might intervene. His brash claim that he could resolve ongoing conflicts in a mere 24 hours was later brushed off as mere sarcasm, exemplifying a pattern of behavior that dismisses the gravity of international relations and the complexities of war.

The implications for America are dire; ignoring these developments could lead the nation down a path that resembles a communist regime, where dissent is stifled and governmental authority is unchecked. Trump's blatant disregard for legal norms is particularly alarming—he has proclaimed himself the chief law enforcer of the Department of Justice, leaving the actual Attorney General effectively mute and compliant with Trump's agenda, rather than fulfilling the duty of upholding justice and the rule of law. This alarming trajectory calls for immediate attention and action to safeguard democratic principles and prevent the erosion of governance in the United States. Donald Trump, during his presidency, was often described as a polarizing figure, with many labeling his actions as erratic or extreme. For instance, his administration's approach to immigration included a policy of mass deportation that sparked significant controversy and legal challenges. In response to these actions, a lawsuit was filed aiming to halt the sweeping deportation efforts.

In the course of the legal proceedings, a judge issued a ruling that mandated an immediate cessation of the deportations. This court order highlighted the necessity for the Trump administration to respond to specific inquiries about the deportation processes being enacted. The ruling underscored concerns about the legality and ethics of the methods employed in the deportation initiative, prompting scrutiny and oversight of the policies during his time in office.

In the recent controversy surrounding immigration policy, a member of Trump's cabinet, known for his aggressive stance on deportation, boldly dismissed a federal judge's ruling. He stated unequivocally that he had no regard for the judge's decision. In response, Trump publicly labeled the judge as a "complete lunatic" and suggested that impeachment proceedings should be considered against him. This rhetoric escalated tensions further, prompting Trump to approach the Supreme Court for intervention.

Chief Justice John Roberts, however, expressed significant discontent with Trump's statements and the actions the president sought to pursue. In a press release addressing the situation, Roberts emphasized the importance of upholding judicial integrity, firmly stating, "For more than two centuries, it has been established that impeachment is not an appropriate response to disagreement concerning a judicial decision. The normal appellate review process exists for that purpose."

These comments underscored the established legal framework that governs the relationship between the executive branch and the judiciary, reinforcing the principle that disagreements with court rulings should be resolved through legal channels rather than through inflammatory rhetoric or threats of impeachment.

In a recent phone conversation, President Trump and President Putin discussed the possibility of implementing a ceasefire amid ongoing tensions between Russia and Ukraine. During this extended two-hour dialogue, Trump advocated strongly for an unconditional and complete cessation of hostilities, emphasizing the need for peace and stability in the region.

However, Putin came to the table with significant and complex demands, reflecting his strategic mindset and his background in the KGB, which has undoubtedly shaped his approach to international negotiations. He presented terms that went beyond a simple ceasefire, indicating his intention to leverage the situation to Russia's advantage.

Despite Trump's optimism and belief that Putin might genuinely agree to the ceasefire proposal, the conversation revealed a stark imbalance in experience and negotiation tactics between the two leaders. Putin, drawing on his extensive political acumen, maneuvered the discussion to extract concessions, effectively taking advantage of Trump's relative inexperience in global diplomacy.

Tragically, shortly after their conversation concluded, reports indicated that Putin's military launched an attack on Ukraine, underscoring the lack of sincerity in his commitments during the call.

This action not only shocked the international community but also confirmed the ongoing distrust between the Ukrainian president and Putin, who remains cautious and skeptical of any overtures for peace from the Russian leader. The situation continues to evolve, with many questioning the sincerity of diplomatic engagements in light of such aggressive military actions.

The president is currently grappling with several challenges, one of which involves proposed budget cuts that could significantly reduce the number of Social Security offices. This decision is particularly concerning for residents in rural areas, where access to essential services is already limited. The potential closure of these offices has sparked widespread unrest, leading to serious protests that have drawn hundreds of concerned citizens. They are voicing their frustrations and urging the administration to reconsider these cuts, highlighting the vital role that Social Security offices play in supporting communities and providing necessary assistance to those in need have gathered at those offices recently.

There have been several Social Security office closures in rural areas as part of a broader effort to streamline operations and reduce costs. Factors like digital transformation and the shift toward virtual services have contributed to these closures. For example, in central Georgia, offices and communities like Thomasville and Vidalia have closed down. Similarly, in North Carolina, offices in Roanoke Rapids, Elizabeth City,

Franklin, and Greenville are among those affected.

These closures pose challenges for individuals in rural areas who may not have reliable Internet access or digital literacy skills to navigate online services while the government aims to improve efficiency. The impact on accessibility to essential services is significant to mitigate these challenges. The Social Security Administration encourages using online services or visiting the nearest open office for assistance. Trump has his hands full; the town hall meeting with voters is not going well. Significant backlash at town halls led to the suspension of these events across the country. Sure, recently, Republican representatives have faced intense backlash at town hall meetings nationwide.

This backlash is linked to efforts by President Trump and Elon Musk to downsize the federal government, which has resulted in many federal employees being fired. Constituents are also worried about the future of Social Security and other social programs. As a result, Republican leaders advised suspending in-person town hall events to avoid confrontations. In the wake of significant policy shifts initiated by President Trump and entrepreneur Elon Musk aimed at downsizing the federal government, a notable number of federal employees have been let go. This wave of dismissals has raised alarms regarding the potential impacts on crucial social safety nets, including Social Security and various welfare programs that millions of Americans rely on. Recently

As a result, town hall meetings hosted by Republican leaders have been marked by heightened tensions. During these gatherings, constituents have voiced their frustrations and concerns with increasing fervor, leading to intense confrontations. The atmosphere at these meetings has often been charged, reflecting the deep-seated anxieties surrounding the future of federal programs that many fear may be compromised.

In light of these escalating conflicts and the unpredictable reactions from their constituents,

Republican leaders have made the strategic decision to suspend in-person town hall meetings across the nation. This pause aims to promote a more controlled environment for discussion and to reassess how party leaders engage with their constituents amid the ongoing debates surrounding federal policies and employee layoffs.

In a prior section of the book, I detailed the significant court order regarding deportations that emerged amid the Trump administration's efforts to expedite the removal of certain individuals from the United States.

Notably, President Donald Trump leveraged the Alien Enemies Act, a rarely invoked law, to hasten the deportation process, specifically targeting Venezuelan gang members. This move was somewhat redundant, as these individuals were already in detention facilities, awaiting their respective court hearings regarding their immigration status.

The Alien Enemies Act has a historical backdrop of being utilized sparingly in the United States, having been applied only three times throughout its history. Its most notorious usage occurred during World War II when it was employed to justify the internment of Japanese Americans, a decision that sparked significant controversy and is now viewed as a grave injustice.

Trump's decision to use this act appeared to stem from his mounting frustration over the perceived sluggishness of deportation rates during his tenure.

Despite his administration's aggressive immigration enforcement policies, a recent report highlighted that the total number of deportations in February fell short compared to those recorded during the Biden administration, even in light of Trump's intensified migrant raids. This inconsistency was likely a contributing factor to his escalating frustrations.

In a decisive move on a Friday afternoon, Trump signed the order to initiate these deportations and publicly announced it the following Saturday. However, his swift actions were met with immediate legal pushback. U.S. District Judge James Boasberg responded quickly by issuing an order that halted the deportations, insisting on taking the time to assess the legality of Trump's actions under the Alien Enemies Act. What exactly is the Alien Enemies Act? It is rooted in history. The Alien Enemies Act of 1798 is part of the United States' Alien and Sedition Acts. It allowed the government to detain and deport non-citizens from hostile nations during times of war or conflict. It is a legal tool that's been around for a while. It's not some extraterrestrial showdown.

The lawsuit that precipitated this judicial intervention was filed by five Venezuelan immigrants, who argued against the legality of their deportations under the new directive. In a remarkable development, the court provisionally converted this individual lawsuit into a class action, effectively blocking the deportation of all non-citizens who fell under the scope of Trump's proclamation.

Judge Bosberg further mandated that any aircraft that had already been prepared to deport these individuals should return to the United States immediately. This swift judicial response underscored the ongoing tensions between executive immigration policies and the judicial system's role in safeguarding the rights of individuals facing deportation.

The more I examine Donald Trump's actions and statements, the clearer it becomes that he may not be fully in touch with the current realities facing the nation and the world.

Throughout both his business career and time in politics, Trump has consistently surrounded himself with individuals who seem to filter information, shielding him from perspectives that might negatively influence his worldview. As Amanda Marconi notes in her analysis for Salon.com, the environment that Trump now operates within the White House is even more insular than during his first administration.

In his previous term, Trump often found himself at odds with several high-profile advisors such as Rex Tillerson, John Bolton, Jeff Sessions, and John Kelly.

These conflicts frequently resulted in their dismissal or resignation. However, this time around, Trump appears to have deliberately avoided appointing individuals who might challenge him or present unwelcome truths. This strategic choice has led to an administration characterized by a lack of dissenting voices.

Marconi highlights that Trump's current isolation from external information is unprecedented; he is spending considerable time in an environment that offers him a steady stream of favorable news and information. This insulated framework may help explain some of the more controversial and factually dubious claims he has made recently.

For instance, he has asserted that egg prices are decreasing, tariff revenues are on the rise, his poll numbers are robust, and the American populace is generally satisfied with the state of current affairs. These assertions, however, do not correspond with the data and reports available to the public.

This tendency to detach from uncomfortable realities seems to be a persistent feature of Trump's approach. The support he receives from his inner circle appears to reinforce his preferences, allowing him to maintain a narrative that is disconnected from information. This raises critical questions about the implications of such isolation, both for Trump himself and for the broader political landscape. As I discussed earlier in the book "Iran and Gaza," we are witnessing a troubling continuation of Donald Trump's aggressive military policies, particularly in the Middle East. Over the recent weekend, U.S. forces conducted a new wave of airstrikes in Yemen that resulted in the death of at least 53 individuals in a relentless campaign targeting the Houthi rebels. This escalation is not isolated; further strikes are anticipated in the coming days, signaling an intention to intensify offensive operations. Trump has shifted away from any facade of defensive action, granting more authority to U.S. Central Command to coordinate these military efforts.

Turning our attention to Iran, Trump has heightened his rhetoric, labeling the Iranian leadership as "sinister mobsters and thugs." He has issued threats of "great force," which starkly contrasts with his earlier campaign promises to end conflicts and minimize U.S. military involvement overseas. This marks a significant departure from his pledges to avoid initiating new wars. Instead, we find ourselves observing a dramatic escalation in military engagements across multiple theaters—Gaza is once again facing a surge in bombing, Yemen is enduring unprecedented airstrikes, and in Ukraine, peace remains a distant dream.

It is disconcerting to see the man who vowed to halt wars from the very first day of his presidency now deeply embroiled in various international conflicts. He is reportedly ordering bombardments with little regard and continues to present himself as some sort of anti-war figure, despite the realities on the ground.

In Gaza, the situation has escalated to alarming levels, with Israel launching its most intense military assault since January, claiming the lives of over 400 people. Israeli Prime Minister Benjamin Netanyahu has justified these actions by stating that the progress towards a durable ceasefire has been insufficient, leading them to resort to bombings as a tactic to break the deadlock. Meanwhile, Trump, who once positioned himself as a neutral broker in these matters, has been notably absent, choosing instead to indulge in golf tournaments and posts on his social media platform, Truth Social, celebrating his victories at Mar-a-Lago.

As the violence continues, Palestinians are being ordered to evacuate their homes amid the chaos, compelling us to ponder whether a full-scale ground invasion is on the horizon. The cycle of bloodshed persists, raising profound concerns about the ongoing humanitarian crisis and the effectiveness of U.S. foreign policy in the region.

The situation unfolding in international politics has raised serious concerns, particularly regarding the stance of President Donald

Trump. Many Americans, in fact, seem to recognize that Trump has aligned himself with individuals who do not embody respect for democratic values or individual rights. One could argue that he is siding with figures that are, at best, questionable in their conduct and, at worst, outright criminal. This alignment raises alarms about the potential consequences for fundamental freedoms in this country.

In recent days, we have witnessed a tragic escalation of violence, particularly in Gaza, where reports indicate that around 400 individuals lost their lives in just the last 24 hours. Simultaneously, the conflict in Ukraine continues to rage on, complicating the international landscape even further. Trump's earlier assertion that he could bring about peace on his first day in office seems increasingly implausible, especially given the ongoing hostilities.

Adding to the complexity of the situation is Trump's relationship with Israeli Prime Minister Benjamin Netanyahu, who is facing significant pressure not only from international observers but also from the plight of hostages who have yet to be released. This presents a rather bleak picture, as both the Israeli and Palestinian populations grapple with the aftermath of the violence.

Moreover, the lengthy conversations Trump had with Russian President Vladimir Putin—reportedly lasting up to hours—suggest a troubling dynamic. It raises questions about the future of Ukraine and underscores a fear that these two leaders could very well negotiate the fate of Ukraine, potentially leading to its further disintegration. The prospect of Trump and Putin agreeing about territorial claims poses an ominous threat, as it may symbolize a dangerous precedent of power politics overriding humanitarian considerations. This ongoing dialogue, or lack thereof, paints a stark picture of what may lie ahead for both Ukraine and broader international relations.

A recent report has emerged detailing a noteworthy phone conversation between former President Donald Trump and Russian President Vladimir Putin, revealing complexities in their long-standing relationship. After years characterized by a close rapport, this particular interaction highlighted a shift in dynamics. Trump reportedly waited for an entire hour before his call was taken, during which time Putin appeared to prioritize other engagements on stage, exhibiting a disregard for the urgency behind Trump's discussion. The primary objective of this call was to negotiate a ceasefire in the ongoing conflict in Ukraine.

When Putin finally answered Trump's call, the tone quickly turned tactical. Trump requested a comprehensive ceasefire in Ukraine, not driven by humanitarian concerns but rather motivated by a desire to achieve a diplomatic success that he could tout publicly. However, Putin's response was far from accommodating; he only agreed to a temporary halt in the targeting of Ukraine's energy infrastructure. Furthermore, he firmly rejected the idea of a complete ceasefire and insisted that the United States halt its military assistance to Ukraine. This critical stipulation was notably omitted from the official White House summary of the conversation, yet it was prominently included in the Kremlin's account, indicating Putin's strategic maneuvering and the leverage he maintained in this dialogue.

The incident starkly reflects the intricate dynamics between the two leaders, with Trump often adopting a tone of deference towards Putin. Historically, Trump has expressed admiration for authoritarian leaders like Putin, frequently underestimating the complexities of international politics and the implications of his own position. This recent exchange serves as a poignant reminder of the pitfalls inherent in such diplomacy, illustrating a recurring pattern of yielding to demands without achieving substantial benefits in return.

Furthermore, this situation prompts broader reflections on public response and civic engagement during periods marked by political inconsistency and uncertainties. The discourse surrounding these developments continues to evolve, inviting deeper scrutiny into the nature of leadership and the intricacies of international relations in an increasingly polarized geopolitical landscape. This conversation not only highlights the immediate geopolitical implications but also raises questions about the long-term consequences of diplomatic strategies based on personal relationships rather than substantive policy considerations.

Recent reports have highlighted significant inaccuracies regarding the representation of notable American figures in military history on official government websites. Notably, the profile of baseball legend Jackie Robinson has reportedly been removed from the Department of Defense's website.

This removal is particularly concerning because it erases a key page dedicated to Robinson's military service during World War II. Previously, an article detailing his time in the Army was accessible, but now it redirects to a page that indicates errors. The updated URL of this page contains "PEI" before the headline, which raises suspicions that it may have been taken down as part of efforts by the Trump administration to eliminate federal programs and information that do not align with their narrative.

Moreover, this incident is not isolated. Recently, there was also controversy surrounding the page dedicated to the Enola Gay, the aircraft that dropped the atomic bomb on Hiroshima. It was taken down, reportedly due to the inclusion of the word "gay" in its title. This has led to concerns that other significant American heroes' contributions to history are being systematically erased or overlooked.

Jackie Robinson stands as a prime example of an American hero, not only for his groundbreaking achievements in baseball but also for his service to the country as a veteran. He was African American. His erasure from the Department of Defense website raises troubling questions about how African American contributions are represented in history.

In addition, we must not forget the contributions of the Native American code talkers during World War II, who played a crucial role in secure communication that the Japanese could not decipher. Their remarkable stories of bravery and dedication are similarly at risk of being overshadowed or forgotten altogether.

The actions taken by this administration and former President Donald Trump seem to reflect a broader agenda to shape historical narratives in a way that minimizes or eliminates credit for diverse contributions. As we confront these challenges, it is imperative that we actively preserve history and acknowledge the truth, continuously working to ensure that the contributions of all American heroes are recognized and celebrated. It is our responsibility to remain vigilant and speak out against any attempts to rewrite history.

Donald Trump exhibits deeply ingrained racist tendencies that have shaped his actions and decisions throughout his career. This pattern is evident in various instances, such as when he automatically removed the accomplished African Americans from prestigious positions only to replace them with white individuals who are often less qualified for those roles.

This behavior highlights a troubling disregard for diversity and meritocracy in leadership. Beyond these racial issues, Trump can be characterized as a perennial loser and a self-sabotaging figure. His destructive tendencies are both innate and apparent; he has a history of undermining not only his own family's business empire but also his relationships. For instance, he has filed for bankruptcy multiple times, notably with two of his casinos, demonstrating his knack for spiraling into financial ruin.

Additionally, his leadership has negatively influenced critical sectors, such as air traffic control, weather forecasting, and firefighting, leading to inefficiencies and disruptions in their essential operations. Despite his grandiose promises of wealth resulting from his controversial trade policies, Trump has instead delivered widespread disappointment and destruction within the economy.

Even those who hope that his trade war will lead to international relations that are more favorable and a change in the behavior of other nations have seen little progress. The reality remains that Donald Trump is perpetually destructive, and this pattern of behavior has defined much of his life, affecting not just himself but also the various sectors and individuals that fall under his influence.

I find myself deeply troubled by the status of America under Donald Trump's leadership. It feels as though our nation has been brought down to an alarming level, and the situation seems to be deteriorating further. I was born in the 1940s, and I have observed Trump's trajectory in public life for many years. I vividly recall when he first attempted to enter the political arena and the fervor surrounding his eventual nomination for his first presidential term. I will never forget the moment he and his close advisor, Steve Bannon, acknowledged the uphill battle ahead, with Bannon remarking that it would take a miracle for Trump to win. To my surprise, Trump himself did not seem convinced he could secure victory.

When the election results were finally announced, and he unexpectedly emerged as the victor, his reaction was akin to that of an excited child. He shouted, "I won! I can't believe I won!" This reaction highlighted a certain naivety about the gravity of the role he was stepping into. Throughout his first term in office, I observed numerous mistakes that suggested he was undergoing a kind of on-the-job training for one of the most powerful positions in the world.

Now, as we enter 2025, Trump has secured a second term as president, and I cannot help but see a troubling transformation. He has learned from his initial time in office, honing his tactics to better serve his interests. It seems evident that he aspires to wield power akin to that of a dictator, systematically dismantling the rule of law and undermining government institutions. The nation is in a state of unrest, yet his supporters stand by him, perhaps clinging to the hope that circumstances will improve. However, the harsh reality is setting in, and there appears to be little that can derail his ambitions.

In my view, the Democratic Party had a critical opportunity to counter Trump's agenda but squandered it. They should have considered shutting down the government to put a halt to his advances, at least temporarily. Moving forward, I foresee more serious errors emerging from Trump in the next six months to a year. To effectively put a stop to his actions, it is essential for Americans to come together. We cannot afford to remain divided along party lines—Democrats versus Republicans—especially in the upcoming midterms.

If the Democrats manage to regain control of the House and Senate, I firmly believe that Trump could face impeachment, as there are valid grounds for such action. It is crucial for us to communicate these issues to the American public; this is the only viable way to halt this reckless trajectory. Our country is facing grave threats, and we are teetering on the brink of another war. As tensions escalate, it appears Trump is attempting to exert control over various regions—whether it be Greenland, the Gaza Strip, the Panama Canal, or even Canada. His rhetoric suggests aggressive ambitions to seize these territories, which, without a doubt, could lead to significant international conflict, as other nations are unlikely to accept such encroachments.

There is an intriguing aspect to Donald Trump's personality that stands out: his tendency to assign nicknames to those he interacts with. He has a penchant for labeling people with terms like "crazy" or referring to judges, rivals, and media outlets as "nasty," a word he seems to favor frequently. This habit reflects a broader strategy in his communication style, where personalization and mockery become tools for political engagement.

However, it is essential to recognize that many across the nation see him differently. A significant portion of the population has dubbed him "Putin's puppet," reflecting their concerns about his apparent admiration for authoritarian leaders. Trump often expresses a desire to emulate strongman figures like Kim Jong-un of North Korea, Xi Jinping of China, and Vladimir Putin of Russia. His fascination with these dictators suggests a longing for power and control that goes beyond conventional presidential aspirations. When he mentioned wanting to act like a dictator from day one, he was not merely jesting; there is an underlying seriousness to his ambitions.

Furthermore, there are troubling allegations regarding Trump's business practices that warrant attention. He has been accused of exploiting his position for personal gain, with reports indicating that he is involved in selling coins as a profit-making venture. This raises numerous ethical concerns about how he intertwines his governmental responsibilities with his business interests. The way he navigates these conflicts of interest calls into question his commitment to serving the public rather than enriching himself.

As these issues unfold, it is imperative for the nation to establish robust leadership within both the House of Representatives and the Senate. The presence of strong political figures who are willing to challenge Trump's actions is crucial for ensuring that accountability and ethics are upheld in governance. Without such leadership, the public may see a continuous cycle of questionable behavior without the necessary checks and balances to address it. The time for decisive and principled leadership is not just important; it is critical for the health of American democracy.

Once again, former President Donald Trump finds himself embroiled in a heated confrontation with a federal judge over a critical immigration issue. He is expected to respond to the judge's demands by noon today. The judge has issued a court order halting the deportations of certain individuals and is seeking clarification on administrative details, such as when the airplane will depart from the local airport to transport detainees. Trump's reaction, however, has been one of blatant defiance; he appears to be disregarding the court's orders, insisting on pushing forward with the deportations despite the judge's ruling.

In an unexpected twist, the Department of Justice (DOJ) is also publicly dissenting against the judge, raising concerns about the integrity of the justice system. It is alarming to witness the U.S. Attorney General acting more like a puppet for Trump than as an impartial enforcer of the law. This dynamic of openly challenging judicial authority has seldom been seen in American history, making it even more troubling. The judge has warned that failure to comply with the court order will lead to severe consequences, yet it seems that Trump remains unbothered, operating under the belief that he is above the law—as if he holds dictatorial power.

On this day, March 20, 2025, Trump is also making headlines by signing an executive order aimed at dismantling the Department of Education. His determination to eliminate this vital institution has been apparent for months, signaling a deep ideological opposition to public education. The Department of Education oversees numerous initiatives that support various demographics, including programs for individuals with disabilities and student loan assistance. By seeking to dismantle the entire department, Trump risks depriving countless Americans of the resources they need to thrive.

His approach raises pressing concerns about the long-term impact on society; many observers are left to wonder about his motivations, considering that education is a powerful tool for empowering individuals and fostering communal growth. Furthermore, the lack of dissenting voices within his administration only exacerbates the situation. There seems to be no one willing to challenge him, even when his actions are detrimental to the country.

Adding to the mounting anxiety, Trump continues to make remarks about the possibility of World War III, leading many to speculate about the global ramifications of his leadership. His belligerent rhetoric poses a serious threat not only to the United States but also to the world at large. In these turbulent times, I find myself sending prayers—not only for our nation but also for the entire planet. It feels as though something must change to halt this troubling trajectory, whether through human intervention or divine means. The need for a solution has never been more urgent as we grapple with the reality of an unstoppable force in Trump's presidency.

As I mentioned earlier in the book about Trump's racism, he just added another outrageous act. Recently, Donald Trump has taken a controversial step by lifting a federal ban that prohibited contractors from establishing segregated facilities, including restaurants, waiting rooms, and drinking fountains. This act has invoked memories of a troubling past in America, raising alarm about the potential return of segregationist practices. It begs the question: where are the Republican leaders in Washington, D.C., to publicly condemn this action?

Specifically, Richard Hudson, as a representative in a district with a significant population of people of color, should be held accountable for his silence. Such actions from Trump are entirely unacceptable, and anyone who chooses to support or remain complicit in this behavior is equally to blame. It is clear that people deserve much better from their leaders.

On another front, Donald Trump recently faced a significant diplomatic setback regarding Iran. In a move, that many believe showcases his shortcomings as a negotiator, Trump sent a meticulously crafted letter to the Iranian leadership, inviting them to engage in discussions toward a nuclear deal. This tactic echoes the successful negotiations initiated by former President Obama, who managed to bring Iran to the table and facilitate a historic agreement. However, Iran's response to Trump was swift and pointed, dismissing his overtures.

Their spokesperson remarked that the insistence of certain "bully states" on negotiations is not aimed at resolving issues but rather imposing their own expectations. The Iranian government made it clear that they would not capitulate to demands made by the United States.

This situation is emblematic because of the broader implications of Trump's foreign policy approach. His record of accomplishment with agreements, such as the U.S.-Mexico-Canada Agreement (USMCA), as well as his handling of the conflict in Ukraine, has left many international actors skeptical of his credibility as a negotiator. In stark contrast, President Obama was able to earn the trust of the Iranian leadership, facilitating an agreement that Trump has since dismantled without a viable replacement, highlighting a stark difference in diplomatic efficacy between the two administrations.

The notion that Trump's unwillingness to engage effectively with leaders from other countries is tied to deeper issues with race is concerning. Some argue that Trump's actions suggest a discomfort or outright antagonism toward people of color, which raises important questions about the implications of his policies and their impact on America is standing in the world. His dismissal of Obama's achievements particularly raises eyebrows, leading many to conclude that Trump's behavior may be driven by more than just political rivalry. Overall, it is disheartening to witness such regression in leadership and the consequences it brings both domestically and internationally.

Ongoing discussions have arisen regarding the motivations behind the recent closures of Social Security offices nationwide. A new memo from Elon Musk has sparked significant concern as it outlines a series of proposed modifications to the existing processes for filing disability and Social Security claims. Among the most notable changes is the requirement that seniors file their claims using paper forms and in person at designated locations. This new directive raises serious questions about accessibility, particularly for the elderly population, who may face mobility challenges or logistical difficulties in accessing these locations.

Additionally, the proposed changes stipulate that individuals with disabilities will need to verify their identity through online platforms. However, this creates an issue for those without reliable internet access, who will be required to travel to a field office to complete this verification in person.

At the same time, there are plans underway to close a significant number of these field offices nationwide, which could lead to a host of complications for those needing to navigate this revised system.

The Social Security Administration (SSA) has projected that the consequences of these changes could force between 75,000 and 85,000 seniors each week to visit the remaining field offices. This influx of visitors, combined with the dwindling number of available offices, is likely to result in exacerbated waiting times and increased obstacles for individuals seeking to obtain their benefits. Many observers deem this approach unacceptable, expressing concern that Musk's actions are intentionally designed to strain the Social Security system, pushing it toward an unsustainable breaking point.

Further compounding this issue are plans for significant layoffs within the Social Security Administration and the closure of numerous field offices, which threaten to undermine the very infrastructure that supports these critical services. Social Security programs are vital lifelines, funded by taxpayer contributions, which provide essential support for millions of Americans. Critics contend that these measures are being implemented primarily to facilitate additional tax breaks for wealthy individuals like Musk, raising ethical questions about the balance of societal responsibility and corporate interests.

In light of these developments, it is crucial for citizens to mobilize, advocate, and utilize all available means to address and oppose these troubling actions, thereby protecting the integrity of the Social Security system.

The issue of racism associated with Donald Trump has reached an alarming level. As a veteran who served in the military, I have firsthand experience with Arlington, Virginia, having been stationed at Arlington National Cemetery. It deeply concerns me that Trump has removed significant information about Black, Hispanic, and female veterans from the cemetery's official website. This action is an egregious display of disrespect and highlights a troubling lack of acknowledgment of the sacrifices made by individuals of color in service to our country.

Trump's behavior displays an astonishing level of contempt for people of color. His actions reflect not just ignorance but profound hostility towards those who are different from him. The toxic misogyny he displays is equally disturbing; it permeates his interactions and rhetoric. His incessant bigotry, coupled with an alarming sense of superiority, reveals a disturbing mindset.

It seems that Trump's animosity has completely blinded him to the basic tenets of humanity and reason. He often reacts with unrestrained hostility when faced with uncomfortable truths, particularly from members of the press. When reporters pose questions that require factual responses, he frequently responds with anger and evasion, opting instead to control the narrative to fit his agenda. This manipulation creates an atmosphere in which serious discourse is often replaced by theatrics.

One of the more troubling aspects of his behavior is how he addresses women in the media. When a female reporter presses him for clarity or challenges him, he resorts to calling her "nasty," a derogatory term that underscores his lack of respect. This pattern extends beyond the press; even when addressing neighbors, he has used similar disrespectful language. For example, he recently referred to one of our Canadian neighbors in an unbelievable and uncalled-for manner, leaving many astonished at his arrogance.

Trump's disdain appears to extend to almost all segments of society, including Congress, judges, and the media. The only individual he seems to genuinely respect and align with is Putin, which is ironic given how often; Putin undermines Trump's credibility on the global stage. Ultimately, Trump's approach to leadership is marked by division and disrespect, which is detrimental not only to our country but to our collective humanity. We deserve a leader who fosters unity and respect for all people, regardless of their background.

Donald Trump has long been accused of corruption, and as he embarked on his second term, many observers argued that his behavior had only deteriorated further. To illustrate this point, I will delve into several significant events that highlight the unusual dynamics of his administration.

As the Commander in Chief, Trump not only holds the highest office in the land but also wields considerable influence over both chambers of Congress—the House of Representatives and the U.S. Senate- where a majority of members are Republicans. It appears that he exerts an overwhelming control over the Republican Party, leading to a concerning lack of independent thought among its members. Rather than engaging in critical analysis or debate, many Republicans seem to follow Trump's directives without question.

Currently, there is a growing perception that Trump is less interested in his presidential duties and more engaged in his personal leisure activities, such as golfing and attending various sporting events. This raises questions about his commitment to governance and the responsibilities of his office.

The interplay between the two major parties becomes particularly evident during legislative votes. When Democrats oppose proposed legislation, the Republicans often rally around Trump's preferences and push the bills through

Congress. This situation underscores how Trump's whims can dictate legislative outcomes, effectively placing his agenda above bipartisanship and critical discourse.

Moreover, there are troubling reports about individuals like Elon Musk, who, despite being a private citizen, has been involved in sensitive government matters. Musk's participation in classified meetings centered on military strategy and cabinet discussions is alarming, as it blurs the lines between private enterprise and governmental affairs, potentially jeopardizing national security.

In summary, the combination of Trump's authoritarian style of leadership within the Republican Party and the unusual influence of private individuals raises significant concerns about the state of governance in the United States.

Trump sits there and signs executive orders; everybody else is running Washington except him. He is getting nowhere with the Ukraine and Russia situation. Do anything anymore. When Trump has a press conference, he does not give the reporters the proper answers when he has asked a direct question, and if he does not like the reporter or the news organization, he bypasses them. He is talking in circles. He is unfair with the press, and now he is aiming at law firms. The problem Trump does not want to govern the United States. This second term is strictly 100% vengeance.

Trump went as far as to Secret Service services from Biden and his family the vice president Harris and other people that he opposed that was in the previous administration he stripped security clearance from the top people that was in the previous administration this has nothing to do with the economy or bring your prices down are to try to solve the Social Security and Medicare and Medicaid problem. He's busy staying in the past fighting anybody you can who went after him when he was in his first term it's an obsession and one thing for sure trump is a bigot and he uses powers to bring down anybody of color especially I wrote about this earlier in my book, at the beginning I probably in the middle of the book, is about the deportation of illegal trump is so twisted and so power hungry, he can't think straight He's getting ready to deport more people.

The Trump administration is now planning to deport more than 530,000 legal immigrants in the United States. You heard that right—legal. Let me explain. This is new reporting from my research. The Trump administration is revoking the legal status of 530,000 Cubans, Haitians, Nicaraguans, and Venezuelans. These immigrants came to the United States <u>legally</u> under the Biden era. That is the problem. Anything Biden did, Trump is going to undo it, regardless of whether it is good or bad, just to keep his name out front like a kid.

Under Biden it was a sponsorship process, and now the Trump administration is urging them to self-deport or face arrest and removal by deportation agents, saying that the termination of their work permits and deportation protections under an immigration authority known as parole. It will take effect in late April, 30 days after March 25, according to a notice posted by the federal government, and the Department of Homeland Security said it would seek the arrest and deportation of those subject to the policy change if they fail to depart the US in the next 30 days. Officials are urging migrants to use the newly repurposed CBP Home smartphone app to register for self-deportation. DHS says it retains the authority to target migrants who arrived under this right before the 30-day period lapses.

Officials say those prioritized for arrest will include migrants who have failed to apply for another immigration benefit like asylum or a green card. In the book, I describe his cabinet personnel who have top positions but are not qualified for the position. Let me tell you what I mean. This is an example. The Department of Defense is a highly important post. This person went through the confirmation process. Many Democrats opposed him because they claimed he was unqualified; he was a television host and a drunken womanizer, drinking on the job, and presented many other negative traits. Trump was not focused on qualifications; he sought loyalty and a yes-man.

The director of the Department of Defense experienced a mishap; he leaked classified information over a chat app, mistakenly texting the classified warrant information to a reporter and some others. This was a significant error at the time. As usual, Trump told the Republicans what to do, and they now assert that there was nothing classified, alleging it is a cover-up. The Senate investigating committee jumped right on this matter and the Democrats were very aggressive because they recognized its seriousness.

Meanwhile, the Republicans and witnesses claim they do not recall any of that. The Democrats made a point that if it is not classified, they should be able to see the documentation, but the Department of Defense refused, asserting that there was no classified information.

The Democrats argued that non-classified documents should be accessible, but the Department of Defense denied this, claiming no information was classified. The department's director, previously known for drinking on the job, is urged to resign by the Democrats. Donald Trump defended him, stating that no classified information was involved. Classified information has restricted access due to its sensitive nature and often pertains to national security as only authorized personnel can view such documents.

The investigating committee is going full speed ahead on this because they got additional information on the mishap that occurred. If the Republicans were on the up-and-up, this could be solved very quickly; they could easily say it was a serious mistake and the director for the volunteer could step down, but he never had a job like this and the prestige. The committee is looking for answers, but when it comes down to one thing, the president has the final word. Trump has no intention to terminate this man because he is loyal and does Trump's will. The investigation committee is working diligently due to the receipt of new information about the mishap.

If the Republicans were transparent, the issue could be resolved swiftly by acknowledging the mistake and allowing the volunteer director to step down. The committee seeks answers, but ultimately, the president has the final say. Trump intends to retain this individual due to his loyalty and alignment with Trump's directives.

The core criticism from the Republican perspective regarding this administration is centered on the perception that accountability is lacking. Many believe that under Trump's leadership, there is a troubling tendency to overlook serious issues and misconduct. It appears that Trump is primarily focused on garnering attention rather than tackling pressing contemporary challenges such as the rising cost of living and gas prices. This behavior leads to concerns about his priorities.

Moreover, there appear to be alarming indicators of a disregard for essential programs, such as Social Security and Medicare. Trump's actions are often characterized by an aggressive approach, which includes targeting various institutions and individuals. He frequently attacks those who hold differing opinions, whether they are his predecessors in office, members of the media, or even judges, attempting to undermine their credibility if they challenge his agenda.

The overarching sentiment is that, rather than moving forward and addressing current issues, Trump appears intent on revisiting past grievances and launching personal attacks, which raises questions about his ability to govern effectively and responsibly in today's complex political landscape. Trump. The focus seems to be primarily on Greenland, Canada, and the Gaza Strip, which appear disconnected from the pressing economic challenges facing the American populace. It raises concerns about his priorities, as he seems absorbed in issues that do not directly address the struggles that many people are experiencing daily.

His singular focus suggests a lack of awareness or concern for the broader implications of current domestic issues. Additionally, as he ages, there are increasing worries about his stability and mental acuity; he often forgets names and struggles to respond coherently to questions posed by reporters. This has led to a growing frustration with his interactions with the press, where he continues to lash out rather than engage constructively.

I have decided to end this chapter of my life, which has involved writing about the bad. As I reflect on my experiences, I realize how memorable they have been. Throughout my lifetime, I have had the privilege of witnessing many presidents come and go, and each one has left a lasting impression on me.

As a former presidential guard in the third Infantry, I can recall numerous moments filled with both joy and sorrow. However, nothing like Trump. As an honor guard, from the excitement of ceremonial duties to the solemn responsibility of ensuring the safety of our leaders, including presidents, every experience has shaped me in profound ways.

It was painful to write about what is happening to our country today. I have encountered unforgettable events that I could write volumes about, but I am concentrating on 2025 only, the Trump administration.

To end my book, I was able to write about many things that were happening in Washington, DC, and the Trump administration, from tense security situations to dismantling and defunding everything in its path and the employment termination of many. Despite the challenges, I had in writing this, I cherish what I was able to accomplish.

Looking ahead, I remain hopeful of a future filled with progress and positive change. I am eagerly anticipating the arrival of a new day, filled with opportunities and the promise of better times.

Make America Great Again was Trump's big lie and con job; it was for white supremacists only. But we, as decent citizens and abiding by the law, can make America great again by believing in God and loving one another, and stop the hatred towards others, such as females, people of color, Asians, and Hispanics. We are all God's children. America will be great and safe when *WE THE PEOPLE* (*noted in the Constitution*) terminate Trump and his corrupt administration forever.

May God keep and bless our Country and keep America the Beautiful once again.

America the Beautiful vs America Not So Beautiful - 2025

www.ingramcontent.com/pod-product-compliance
Lightning Source LLC
Chambersburg PA
CBHW041038050426
42337CB00058B/4964